I Belong

Preparing for my First Holy Communion

In the name
of the
Father

My name is

-- -- -- -- -- -- -- -- -- -- -- -- --

-- -- -- -- -- -- -- -- -- -- -- -- -- -- -- --

Names

Names are very special.
It is good when we know one another's names.

My friends' names are

....

....

....

If I had a pet spider I would **call** it

- - - - - - - -

If I had a pet lion I would **call** it

- - - - - - - -

My family, my catechist, and I, will all get to know and love Jesus more this year.

My catechist's name is _____

I have a prayer sponsor who is praying for me.
My prayer sponsor is called _____

The Bible

The Bible tells us about God and about us. It tells us how to live as the People of God.

The Old Testament

The Old Testament is the first part of the Bible. It was written long before Jesus was born. Here is a story from the very beginning of the Old Testament. It is about Adam naming the animals.

God made out of the earth all the wild animals and all the birds of heaven. God brought them all to the man to see what he would call them. Whatever the man called each living creature, that was its name.

4

(Genesis 2:19-20)

Draw some of your favourite animals. Write their names.

People wanted to give God a name.
They said ... God is a kgni
They said ... God is a jdgeu
Jesus came to tell us God is a
loving parent

New Testament

The angel said to Mary,
"You will bear a son, and you will
give him the name Jesus.
He will be great and will be called
the Son of the Most High."
(Luke 1:31-32)

The New Testament is the second part of
the Bible. It has stories about Jesus in it.
In the New Testament we hear that Mary
was going to have a baby and she was to
call him Jesus.

When Jesus grew up he was baptised in the River Jordan. He heard a voice from heaven saying,

"This is my beloved Son. I am delighted with him."

Here is the whole story of the baptism of Jesus.

John the Baptist was baptising people in the River Jordan. People used to be baptised in those days to show they were sorry for their sins. Jesus had never done anything wrong, but he waded out into the river and asked John to baptise him.

At first John didn't want to baptise him, but Jesus insisted.

Jesus wanted to be baptised as a sign that he was starting a new way of life. He went down under the water as if he were drowning, and then came up for breath. All of a sudden something wonderful happened. The heavens opened, and the Spirit of God came to Jesus in the form of a dove.

Then everyone heard a voice like thunder.

The voice said,

"This is my beloved Son. I am delighted with him."

(Adapted from Matthew 3:13-17)

Colour this picture of Jesus being baptised in the River Jordan by John the Baptist.

Church

I was baptised at

- - - - - - - - - - - - - - Church.

When I was baptised the priest said to me,

" - - - - - - - - - - - ",

I baptise you in the NAME of the Father and of the Son and of the Holy Spirit."

When I was baptised God said to me,

" - - - - - - - - - - - - ,
You are my beloved child. I am delighted with you."

When I go to church I dip my finger in the Holy Water and say, "In the name of the Father and of the Son and of the Holy Spirit."

This is to remind me of my

- - - - - - - - - - - - - - - - - - - -

When I go to the Eucharist I will remember that my baptism links me up with everyone else in church.

We are all baptised.

We are all beloved children of God. We can all say together:

Our Father, who art in heaven, hallowed be thy name. Thy kingdom come. Thy will be done on earth, as it is in heaven. Give us this day our daily bread, and forgive us our trespasses as we forgive those who trespass against us, and lead us not into temptation, but deliver us from evil.

9

Everyday Life

The story of Adam tells us that God makes us all, and gives us this beautiful world to care for.

Jesus shows us how to live as children of God.

I can <u>live</u> like a beloved child of God because I <u>am</u> a beloved child of God.
I have the Holy Spirit with me just as Jesus did.

This month I am going to live like a child of God by …

— —

Find all these words about God our Father.

Kind generous **patient**
loving **thoughtful** fun
wonderful caring

G	E	N	E	R	O	U	S	P	T	N	E	I	T	A	P
N	N	U	Z	Y	P	L	U	F	T	H	G	U	O	H	T
I	I	I	G	D	O	M	F	R	I	X	K	K	I	N	D
V	H	E	R	P	P	S	W	R	N	A	E	I	H	G	D
O	D	F	W	A	G	H	A	Y	U	K	Y	N	D	C	V
L	E	H	C	N	C	C	L	U	F	R	E	D	N	O	W

I have called you by your name.
You are mine.

(Isaiah 43:I)

Stick
a
photo
of
yourself
here

This is your page for adding your own ideas. You can use it for drawing pictures, or writing prayers. You might like to stick in a photograph of your baptism.

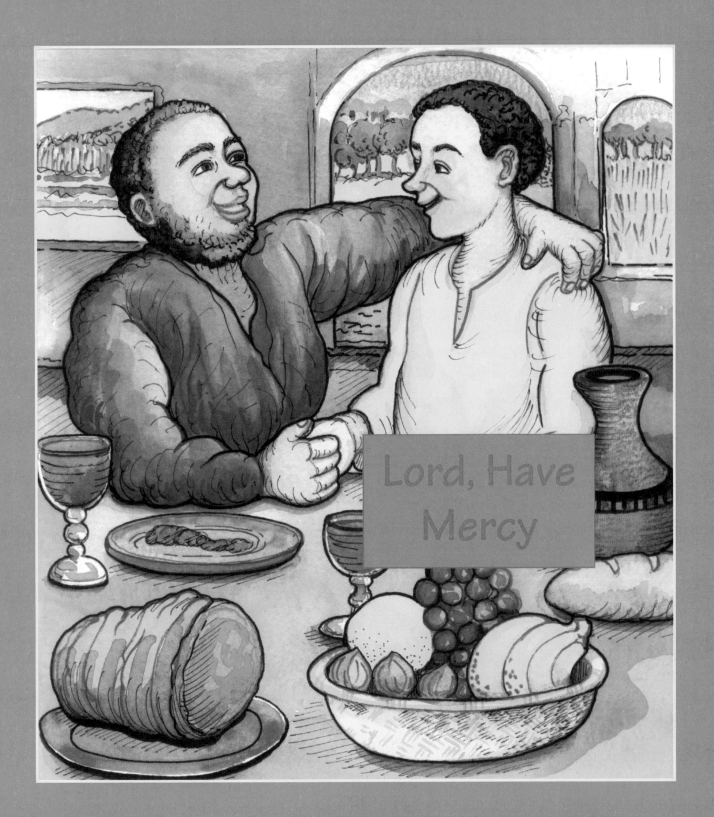

Here is a story about a girl who owned a kitten.

Katie had a for her birthday, but the kitten wouldn't go near her. It hid under the

"Poor thing!" said Katie. "You're cold." And she gave him a

Still the kitten wouldn't go near her. "Poor thing!" said Katie. "You're thirsty." And she gave him a of

The little kitten still hid. Was Katie angry? Oh no! "Poor thing!" she said. "You're hungry." And she gave him some

And still the little kitten hid. Katie loved her little kitten.

"Poor thing!" she said. "You're very, very frightened."

She gently picked him up and stroked him and stroked him until his little stopped beating wildly.

"I'm going to call you

--------------------," she said.

And  purred and purred.

If you had a kitten that wouldn't go near you, what would you do? Would you still love it?

Perhaps you have a pet that was naughty. Tell your friends what the pet did. Do you still love your pet?

Perhaps you are naughty sometimes. Do the grown-ups you belong to still love you?

Draw a picture showing that your family still loves you even after you have been naughty.

Old Testament

Last session we talked about the wonderful world God made, and how wonderfully WE are made. But even so, there is a lot of unhappiness in the world. Here is a very old story, written before Jesus was born, that explains why people can be full of hope, even though things seem to go wrong.

Adam and Eve lived in a beautiful garden where there were all sorts of wonderful fruits to eat. God said they could eat anything they liked, but there was one tree that they mustn't eat the fruit of, because if they did it would kill them.

Now the snake was the craftiest of all the creatures in the garden. He hated the man and woman. He slithered up to Eve and told her that if she ate this she would live for ever. Eve ate the fruit, and gave some to Adam. Straight away they were very frightened, and hid away from God. God was very sorry that the man and woman had harmed themselves. From now onwards people would always have to work hard, and suffer, and die. But God had a wonderful idea.

God promised that one day another woman would have a son, and he would SAVE the world from despair. From then on, people waited for this SAVIOUR. God kept reminding people about the great PROMISE until at last the PROMISE was kept.

(Adapted from Genesis 3)

We know the promise has been kept. The person who came to save us was

Jesus

New Testament

When Jesus grew up he told lots of stories to teach us about God.

What does this one tell us about God?

The Story of a Forgiving Father

There was once a father who had two sons. The younger son was fed up working for his father, and he asked if he could have his share of the money NOW. The father sadly gave his son the money. Off went the son to a faraway country. He bought good clothes, he made lots of friends, and gave lots of parties.

After a while he ran out of money and his friends left him. To make matters worse a terrible famine hit the country. The younger son was starving. He managed to get some work, but it wasn't very nice! He had to look after some pigs! He was so hungry he wanted to eat the pig food, but no one offered him any.

At last the younger son came to his senses. "Even my father's servants are better off than this," he said. "I'll go back and say I'm sorry. I'll say I'm not good enough to be his son, so please could I be his servant. Then I'll get some good food again."

He trudged along, practising what he would say to his father. His father saw him coming while he was still a long way off, and ran out to meet him joyfully.

"Quick!" the father shouted to the servants. "Get some fine clothes for my son. Get a ring for his finger and sandals for his feet. Kill the fatted calf and let's have a party. My son was lost but he is found. I thought he was dead but he's alive."

Meanwhile the elder son was coming back from working in the fields. He was so jealous when he discovered what all the fuss was about.

"I've been working all hours for you," he grumbled, "and you've never had a party for me. But now here comes your good-for-nothing son, and you kill the fatted calf. It's not fair."

"My son, you know that all I have is yours," said the kind father. "I love you both. But it is only right that we should celebrate now. For my son was lost but now he is found. He was dead, but now he is alive."

(Adapted from Luke 15:11-32)

Colour this picture of the Forgiving Father.

When we go to the Eucharist we are like the younger son who came to his senses.
God is like the loving father in the story – delighted to see us.

God is always full of love.

At the Eucharist we remember the times we have been like Adam and got things wrong.
We remember the times we have been like the younger son before he came to his senses.

We also remember

God is always full of love.

We say,

Lord, have mercy.

Mercy is a very special kind of love. Mercy is

kindness   **understanding**   forgiveness   **patience**

God showed mercy to the first people and promised a Saviour.
The father showed mercy to the younger son and gave him a party.
God our loving Father shows us mercy, and at the Eucharist God gives us special food.
This food is Jesus the Saviour, the Bread of Life. It gives us the strength to live as the children of God.

Everyday Life

Every time we show mercy, no matter how angry we feel inside, we are learning to be more like God who is always loving and merciful.

How can we show mercy

at home?

at school?

Find the words:

MERCY LOVE PATIENCE KINDNESS LORD FATHER

R	P	D	K	M	E	R	C	Y	O	P	H	J	K	L	G
E	N	U	Z	Y	P	L	U	F	T	H	G	U	O	O	T
H	I	I	D	S	S	E	N	D	N	I	K	K	I	V	D
T	H	E	R	R	P	V	W	R	N	A	E	I	H	E	D
A	D	F	W	A	O	O	A	Y	U	K	Y	N	D	C	V
F	E	H	C	N	C	L	L	E	C	N	E	I	T	A	P

Here is a prayer to say. Choose a word to fill in along the dotted lines. Choose something you would like God to help you with.

Dear Father in heaven,

Thank you for your MERCIFUL LOVE.

Help me to be more .... in future.

I ask this through Jesus Christ

your Son.

Amen.

Don't forget you can add as much as you want to your file each month.

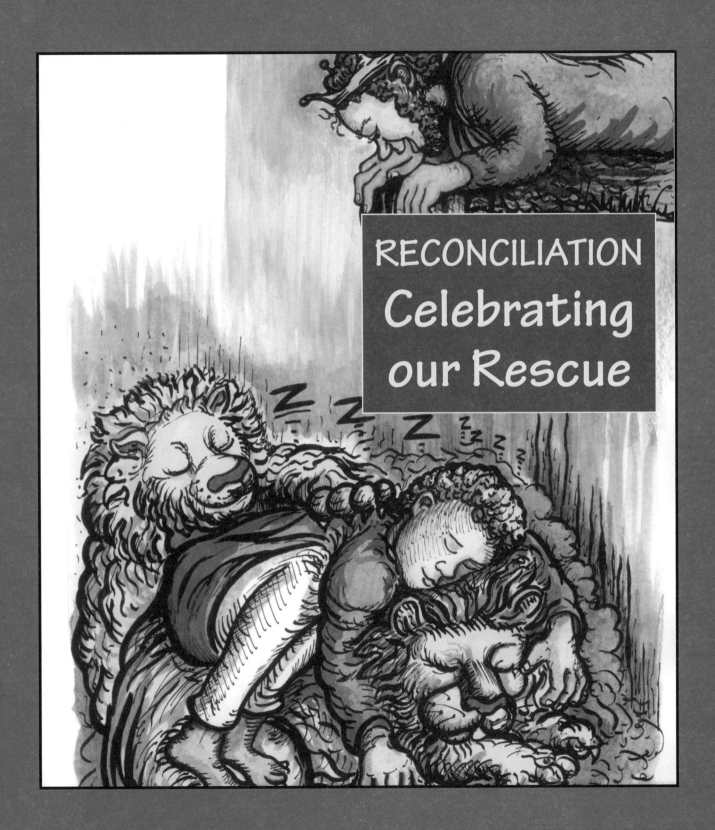

RECONCILIATION
Celebrating
our Rescue

HIJACKED PLANE LATEST!

EVERYONE RESCUED

"WE ARE DELIGHTED," say families

LOST CHILD RESCUED FROM MOUNTAIN LEDGE

PARENTS OVERJOYED

Have you ever rescued anything that you love very much?
Was it very difficult?

Have you ever seen anyone rescued from a fire or water or from a road accident?
Tell everyone about it.

Perhaps you have been in trouble or danger?
Who saved you?
How did you feel afterwards?

Draw a picture of someone being rescued.
It could be a rescue from a fire, or from a storm at sea.

Old Testament

There are lots of "Rescue" stories in the Old Testament. Here is one about Daniel rescued from the lions' den.

There was once a brave young man called Daniel. Some men were jealous of Daniel, but they couldn't get him into trouble because he was so good. The bad men thought of a trick.

They got the king to agree that anyone who prayed to God should be thrown into a pit of lions. The king agreed because he didn't know about the One True God.

Daniel went on praying to God, and the bad men told the king. The king was very sad. He knew Daniel was a good man, but he had to keep his word. He threw Daniel into the lions' den. In the morning the king went to the lions' den. There he saw something wonderful. Daniel was alive. Daniel told the king that God had RESCUED him because he had trusted in God. After that the king believed in God. He told the whole world that Daniel's God was full of power. Daniel's God SAVES and RESCUES.

(Adapted from Daniel 6)

New Testament

Jesus wanted to tell us how God is always ready to RESCUE us.

He made up stories to help us realise it.

You have already heard the story of the Forgiving Father. When the younger brother came home the father rescued him from hunger and poverty. He even gave him a party, because he was so glad his son was found.

Here is another story Jesus told.

There was once a shepherd who had a hundred sheep. Every night he counted them carefully as he put them into the sheepfold. One evening when he counted, he noticed that one was missing. He knew who it was, as he knew them all by name. It was one of the little lambs.

He decided to go out and look for it, because there was great danger on the hillside. It might fall down a cliff, or be eaten by wild animals. Once he saw that the other sheep were safely in the fold, he set off to look for his lost lamb. It grew darker and darker, but still he kept on looking, and calling out for his lost lamb.

He heard the wild animals growling, and felt the wind growing stronger and stronger, but he would not give up hope. At last, near the edge of a cliff, he heard a frightened bleat. It was his lost lamb. Carefully, he climbed down to where the lamb had fallen, and RESCUED it.

He gently put it over his shoulders and carried it back to the fold. Then the shepherd called his friends and neighbours. "Let's celebrate," he said, "for I have found my lost sheep."

(Adapted from Luke 15:4-7)

Colour this picture of the Good Shepherd finding his lost sheep.

We are just like the people that heard the stories Jesus told. We are children of God, and we are full of love and joy and wonderful feelings. But sometimes we have other feelings that are not very nice.
We might feel

• angry • spiteful • greedy • jealous • crafty

God gave us these feelings too! Feelings are very useful, because they tell us what we need.

If I feel hungry I need .... dofo

If I feel lonely I need a .... frenid

If I have nasty feelings I know I need someone to RESCUE me.
I am like the lost sheep that couldn't RESCUE itself.
Sometimes I feel really lost and helpless.
My feelings take me over.
But God is my RESCUER.
When I feel lost and helpless God comes to my RESCUE and saves me.

Here am I with a friend sorting things out with God's help.

When we have sorted it out we have been RECONCILED.

RECONCILIATION

is happening all the time in our lives. Every time we sort things out with our parents, teachers, and friends, we are being RECONCILED.

We go to RECONCILIATION to CELEBRATE all the times we forgive each other.

We go to RECONCILIATION to CELEBRATE all the times God forgives us.

Life is full of RECONCILIATION, so life is full of CELEBRATION.

When you go to RECONCILIATION in church you are CELEBRATING with all the people of God.

The priest is standing in for them. The priest is also standing in for God.

When you talk to the priest during RECONCILIATION it is YOUR SPECIAL TIME.

Nobody else knows what you are saying to him. What you say is between YOU and GOD.

You can say ANYTHING to the priest, because in RECONCILIATION you are really talking to God your loving RESCUER.

One of the things you could say is…

I have come to thank God who forgives me for……………………………………

(and then say something you did or said that you know was deliberately unloving).

Reconciliation isn't just about CELEBRATING our rescue in the past. It is also about getting help for the future.

In the Sacrament of RECONCILIATION God gives us hope and strength for problems that still aren't sorted out.

We promise that, with God's help, we will be more loving in future

to ourselves,

to others,

and to God.

We will think more about this next time we meet.

And finally, here comes the Word Search! A harder one this time! Find these words:

JOY RELIEF FORGIVENESS
RESCUED LOVE HELP
STRENGTH SORRY CELEBRATION

```
F  J  K  L  O  V  E  Y  R  W  Q  O  O  I  A  B
O  I  Z  B  E  E  F  N  M  J  F  E  I  L  E  R
R  S  P  L  K  M  B  G  T  W  S  Z  T  P  X  E
G  Z  T  X  C  V  B  N  M  Y  L  K  Y  L  H  S
I  M  N  R  B  X  Z  W  Q  O  T  P  J  E  G  C
V  T  R  H  E  K  L  Y  O  J  O  Y  L  T  Y  U
E  C  V  B  N  N  Q  H  G  O  F  P  N  R  L  E
N  E  E  R  R  N  G  M  K  Y  Y  Y  B  W  K  D
E  T  G  O  N  O  I  T  A  R  B  E  L  E  C  M
S  K  L  P  Y  T  F  G  H  V  B  S  W  T  U  H
S  O  R  R  Y  K  L  P  H  H  A  E  I  V  C  G
```

Are you lost with the Word Search?
Do you need RESCUING?
Ask someone to help!

This is your page for using at home. You might like to draw some pictures of you doing some loving things for God and people. You might like to write a prayer thanking God for rescuing you when you did something unkind.

Everyday Life

Is there anything you really wanted to do when you were younger, but it was too difficult?

Here I am getting something wrong to start with

Who helped you to get it right in the end?

The people you live with care for you. If you are frightened of something, like learning to swim, or being in the Class Assembly, they will encourage you to have a go.
When they trust you with things, like important messages, or keeping an eye on the baby, it helps you believe in yourself, because they believed in you first.

Here I am being helped by someone to GET IT RIGHT

Jesus was always helping people "GET IT RIGHT".
He did this through the stories he told.
Can you remember two of the stories we have talked about?

Fill in the missing letters

The PR • D • G • L S • N

The L • ST SH • • P

Jesus didn't only make up stories to help us. Everything he did in his life shows us how much God loves us. Here is how Jesus treated a bad man that nobody liked.

ZACCHAEUS – THE MAN JESUS BELIEVED IN

Zacchaeus was a mean, greedy man. He had hardly any friends because all he cared about was money.
One day he heard Jesus was coming to town.
He was very curious about him, and decided to go along and see him.
Now, Zacchaeus was very short, and there were lots of people crowding around. They wouldn't let Zacchaeus get to the front. Jesus was coming nearer, and Zacchaeus gave up all hope of seeing him.
Suddenly he had an idea. There was a sycamore tree nearby.
He decided he would climb the tree. He didn't care if the people laughed at him. He would have a really good view of Jesus.
Imagine his surprise when Jesus stopped beneath the tree!
Jesus looked up at him and smiled.
"Come down, Zacchaeus," said Jesus. "I'd really love to have a meal with you today."
Zacchaeus was thrilled to hear such good news. He knew he had treated people badly by cheating them out of their money.
That was why he had hardly any friends.
It was amazing that Jesus actually wanted to come to his house.

As Jesus and Zacchaeus chatted, something strange happened. Money didn't seem so important to Zacchaeus any more. It was much more fun talking to Jesus. Zacchaeus began to realise how lonely he had been.

He felt sorry about what he had been like in the past, but he knew that he had changed. Jesus cared for him, and that made all the difference.

"I know what I'll do," he told Jesus.

"I'll give half my money away to the people who really need it, and if I've cheated anyone, I'll give them back four times as much as I took from them."

(from Luke 19:1-9)

In what way did Zacchaeus change? Why did he decide to be generous to his neighbours?

Colour this picture of Jesus helping Zacchaeus to "GET IT RIGHT".

Jesus is with us in a special way in the Sacrament of Reconciliation, just as he and Zacchaeus were together long ago.
We can't see Jesus now, so the priest takes his place.
Zacchaeus loved talking to Jesus. He told him all the things he couldn't tell anyone else, because he knew Jesus would understand.

We can tell the priest anything we are ashamed about, or that we would like to put right. The priest is there to show us Jesus' understanding and love.

HERE IS A RECONCILIATION PRAYER.

O my God,
thank you for your forgiveness.
I know you love me even when I am unloving.
Please help me to live like Jesus and to forgive others as you forgive me.

Remember that what you say is a secret between you and Jesus. The priest can't tell anyone what you tell him, because he is only standing in for Jesus.

We go to Reconciliation for God's help. God can help us put things right.

Perhaps you could make up a better prayer. You could say this prayer before you go to sleep at night, and before you go to Reconciliation.

Here is a picture of me, saying that with God's help
I will be more loving in future.
You can draw yourself sitting or kneeling at Reconciliation.

THE SACRAMENT OF RECONCILIATION

BEFORE THE SACRAMENT

Think back over the good times and the bad times you have had lately.
Thank God for the good times. Even the bad times probably had some
good bits. It is good to make up with someone we have had a row with.
We can go to Reconciliation to CELEBRATE these good bits.
Sometimes we haven't been able to put the bad things right.
We can go to Reconciliation to get help for these things.
Talk to God in your heart about these things.

DURING THE SACRAMENT

Tell the priest how long it is since you last went.
(You can't do this at your First Reconciliation!)
Tell him what you want to tell Jesus – the things you need help with.
LISTEN to what the priest says to you. He will ask you to say a little
prayer or do something kind during the week, to show your
love of God and of everyone else.
LISTEN CAREFULLY to the wonderful words of forgiveness he says.
We know God always forgives us,
but it is good to hear it put into words.

AFTER THE SACRAMENT

Thank God for the chance to celebrate Reconciliation. If the priest
asked you to say a prayer, say it straight away before you forget.
This is called your PENANCE.
Say a prayer for the priest.

THANKS BE TO GOD

Find the names of these people in the Bible whom God
helped to get it right.
Then look up their stories in the Bible.

PETER   MARY MAGDALENE
ZACCHAEUS   PAUL
THE GOOD THIEF

F P L E N E L A D G A M Y R A M
T H E G O O D T H I E F I L E R
R S P L K M B G T W S Z T P X E
G Z T X C V B N M Y L K Y L H T
I M N R B X Z W Q O T P J E G E
V T S U E A H C C A Z Y L U A P

Remember: This is YOUR page.

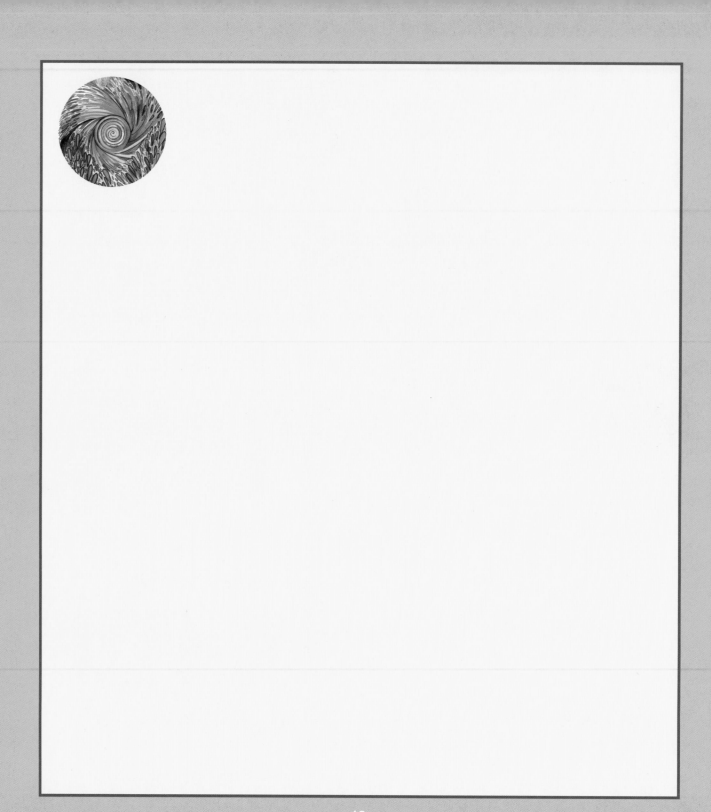

Everyday Life

Here are two special experiences that might happen to you one day.

Which one do you prefer?

The firework display was the best Sarah had ever been to. Rockets zoomed into the sky and showered silver stars above the trees. Catherine Wheels whizzed round and round, and Golden Fountains rained sparkling jewels everywhere.

Andrew felt his heart pounding as he raced for the ball. He reached it just before his opponent, and kicked it with all his might. "Yes!" shouted Andrew. "GOAL!" roared the crowd. In the last minute of play Andrew had scored. His team had won the cup!

Perhaps you have had a much better special experience. Perhaps you dream about something full of glory?

Draw a picture of a glorious experience you have had.

All special experiences are gifts from God. Sometimes they are wild and exciting. Sometimes they are peaceful and dreamy. Sometimes the most ordinary things seem somehow different and glorious. All these experiences come from God who makes everything. They all show the GLORY OF GOD.

Old Testament

In the Old Testament there were people who had very special experiences of God. They could see the GLORY OF GOD.

Moses was one of these people. (You might know the story of when he was a baby and his mother hid him in the river to save his life. Ask someone to tell you the story if you don't know it.)

Here is the story of a very important experience of the glory of God that Moses had.

Moses used to look after his father-in-law's sheep. One day he led the flock right into the middle of the desert until he came to the great Mount Horeb. All of a sudden he saw something very strange. There was a GLORIOUS bush nearby that was blazing with light. The bush was on fire! What was so strange about it was that although the bush was burning brightly, it was not being burnt up. It just blazed and blazed with the most GLORIOUS light. Moses wondered what he should do. The burning bush was so strange it was frightening, but it was so beautiful he wanted to go nearer. As soon as he plucked up courage to go nearer he heard a voice calling him.

"Moses! Moses!"
"Here I am!" said Moses.
The voice said, "Do not come any closer, and take off your sandals. You are standing on HOLY GROUND."
The voice went on to say,
"I am the God of your father, the God of Abraham, the God of Isaac, the God of Jacob."
Moses hid his face, for he didn't dare look into the face of God. God told Moses to save his people from the wicked Pharaoh. Moses was to be their SAVIOUR, and lead them out of slavery, and into freedom, to a Promised Land. In this land there would be food and drink for everyone. It would be flowing with milk and honey!

(adapted from Exodus 3:1-6)

New Testament

For hundreds of years people waited for God to send a Saviour. WE know that God's glorious plan was to become a human being, but in those days nobody knew. They just waited and waited.

They waited for a GLORIOUS .... KNGI

They waited for a GLORIOUS .... LEDREA

They waited to see the glory of God in powerful and mighty signs.

Mary waited for a tiny baby. She knew that the Glory of God would be hidden in her little son.

You know the story of how God kept the GLORIOUS promise. Jesus was born in a stable at Bethlehem.
Here is the story of how some shepherds were the first to hear the GOOD NEWS. The quiet glory of Jesus' birth.

Just outside Bethlehem there were some shepherds up in the hill tops. They were guarding their sheep from the wolves and other wild creatures, but it was a peaceful sort of night with nothing much happening.

All of a sudden an angel of the Lord stood by them, and the glory of God shone round about them. They were very, very frightened. But the angel said to them,

"Do not be afraid. I have some great news for you, and for everybody. For today in Bethlehem a SAVIOUR is born, who is CHRIST THE LORD. And this shall be a sign for you.
You will find the baby wrapped in swaddling clothes and lying in a manger."

And suddenly there was a whole crowd of angels GLORIFYING God and singing,

"GLORY TO GOD IN THE HIGHEST AND PEACE TO GOD'S PEOPLE ON EARTH."

After the shepherds had seen the baby they went away glorifying and praising God and telling everyone they met what had happened.

The shepherds saw the GLORY of GOD on the hillside and the GLORY of GOD in the manger. What was the same about each kind of glory? What was different?

Colour this picture of the shepherds seeing the Glory of God.

A SAVIOUR IS BORN

When we go to church for the Eucharist we are like the shepherds seeing the glory of God. Sometimes we can experience the glory. Usually it is hidden. At some Eucharists we have a chance to sing the song of glory and praise the angels sang.

praise

OOH!

Glory to God in the highest, and peace to his people on earth. Lord God, heavenly King, almighty God and Father, we worship you, we give you thanks, we praise you for your glory.

Lord Jesus Christ, only Son of the Father, Lord God, Lamb of God, you take away the sin of the world: have mercy on us; you are seated at the right hand of the Father: receive our prayer. For you alone are the Holy One, you alone are the Lord, you alone are the Most High, Jesus Christ, with the Holy Spirit, in the glory of God the Father. Amen.

GLORY

GURGLE gurgle

WOW

BOW-WOW

Alleluia!

YAP

Draw three things that make you want to glorify God.

Find the following words in the Word Search:

GLORY   PRAISE   HONOUR   ADORE

SUPER   HOSANNA   THANKS   GREAT

A	H	O	S	A	N	N	A	K
X	P	R	A	I	S	E	L	H
N	S	X	Y	R	O	L	G	J
U	U	S	K	N	A	H	T	R
Y	P	G	R	E	A	T	M	S
D	E	H	O	N	O	U	R	O
G	R	X	E	R	O	D	A	A

This space is for your own ideas. You might like to stick in some glorious pictures from a magazine.

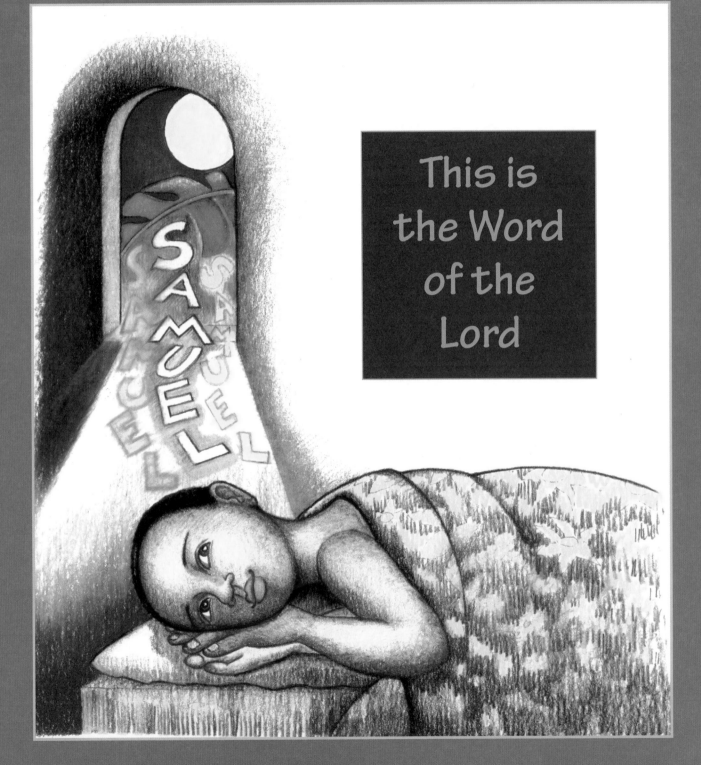

Do you know a good story?

Everyday Life

What is missing from these animals?
Draw them in.
How well would the animals survive without them?

Here are some SOUND words.
See if you can find the same words in the Word Search.

CRACKLE   FIZZLE   POP   BUZZ
WHOOSH   MIAOW   PING

C	R	A	C	K	L	E
M	P	K	J	X	B	L
I	I	L	A	U	H	Z
A	N	K	Z	G	Q	Z
O	G	Z	P	O	P	I
W	H	O	O	S	H	F

How well would you survive if you didn't
listen to the people who care for you?

Easily?   With difficulty?   Not at all?

Tell the group about a time you were glad
you listened.

Old Testament

Last time we talked about wonderful
things. Sometimes they were grand and
showy. Other times they were quiet and hidden. Here is a wonderful
story about a young boy listening to God in the quiet of the night.
*(Samuel was a very special child. His mother, Hannah, had prayed to
God for a baby for years. She promised God that if she had a baby,
she would let him serve God in the temple when he was old enough.
God heard Hannah's prayers, and eventually Samuel was born.)*

When Samuel was still a young
boy he went to live and work in
the temple.
He helped the old priest Eli,
who was going blind.
One night when it was very quiet he
<u>heard</u> a voice calling him. He thought
it was Eli, so he jumped up and
ran to him.
"I didn't call you," said Eli.
"Go back to bed."
Samuel went back to bed, but he
<u>heard</u> the voice calling him again.
He jumped up and ran to Eli.

"Here I am. I HEARD you call me,"
said Samuel.

"I didn't call you," said Eli. "Go back to bed."

Samuel went back to bed, very puzzled.
He was just falling asleep when he <u>heard</u> the voice
call him for the third time. Up he jumped and ran to Eli.

"You did call me," he said. "I <u>HEARD</u> you."
This time Eli realised that it was God calling Samuel.

"Go back to bed," he said.
"If you <u>hear</u> the voice again, say,
'Speak, Lord, for your servant is <u>listening</u>.'"

Samuel lay down and <u>listened</u> in the silence.
It was a very special time.
Once again God called Samuel.

"SAMUEL! SAMUEL!"

Full of wonder, Samuel said,

"Speak, Lord, for your servant is <u>listening</u>."

God gave Samuel a message for Eli.
It was the first message that Samuel <u>heard</u> from God.
When he grew up he often <u>heard</u> messages from God, and he
passed them on to anyone who would <u>listen</u>.

New Testament

At last, the time came for Jesus to be born. (Do you remember that the New Testament is all about Jesus?)

God could have arranged for Jesus to be born anywhere.

He could have been born in a .... plcaae.

He was born in a .... stblea.

He could have been born very......................... irch.

He was born very......................... ropo.

He could have been born in splendour and loud glory.
He was born in the quiet glory of the night.

JESUS IS THE WORD OF GOD

At Christmas God's promise was kept.

JESUS

was born in a quiet stable in Bethlehem.
Jesus is the

WORD OF GOD

Colour this picture of the WORD OF GOD born in a stable.

66

Church

Two thousand years ago, the WORD OF GOD lived with us as a human being. People could listen to him as he spoke. Jesus is still with us today in many different ways. One of the ways he is with us is in the readings at Mass. When we listen to them we are listening to the WORD OF GOD.

The first reading is from the Old Testament, and we hear about the times when people were still waiting for the Saviour.

After the first reading we say, "Thanks be to God."

The Psalms are hymns of praise. Jesus loved to sing these.

The second reading is often from a letter the early Christians used to listen to. After we listen to it we say, "Thanks be to God."

In the Gospel we hear stories about the life of Jesus. After hearing the Gospel we say, "Praise to you, Lord Jesus Christ."
This is because the Gospel is .... (ogdo wens)

Draw you listening to something or someone special. It might be in church, at home, on holiday, or anywhere.

Everyday Life

Here is a game for you to play. When you play it with your catechist you can all move when the catechist throws the dice. When you play it at home everyone can take turns at throwing the dice. I wonder if the best listener will always win!

4 Listen to birds sing. FORWARD 4	5	12 Hear good idea. FORWARD 6	13	21
	6		14	20
3	7	11	15	19 Hear favourite group. GO FORWARD 2
2	8	10	16	
1 START	9 Listen to good story. GO FORWARD 2		17	18

22

Listen to bad idea.
GO BACK 3

29

30

38

Don't listen to teacher. GO BACK 4

28

31

37

39

23

27

32

Don't listen to parent. GO BACK 5

36

40

24

26

35

41

25

Hear Bible story.
GO FOWARD 6

33

34

42

HOME

This page is for your own ideas. You could write a "thank you" prayer for things you like listening to. You could stick in pictures of things that make lovely sounds. How about sausages sizzling in a pan, or your favourite group?

Bread to Offer

Once there was a little The  shone and made it grow.

It grew into a fine wheat plant with hundreds of

The  came and cut down the wheat.

She took it to the  to be ground into

The flour was taken to the to be baked into

A big  took it to the

Someone bought the bread and took it home for the

They made sandwiches and had a great

Who gets the food in your house?
Who prepares it?
Do you help?

Draw you preparing a meal with people you like. It might be a picnic, or a birthday party, or just a meal you had when everyone was really hungry.

Old Testament

Do you remember a while ago we were talking about Moses?

He saw the glory of God in a burning bush, and God told him to save the Israelites from the wicked Pharaoh who was using them as slaves.

Moses listened to God and led the slaves out of Egypt.

Moses and his people wandered in the desert for forty years, waiting for God to lead them into the Promised Land.

At first the people knew very little about God. They had to learn to trust God and to love one another. They had to learn that they were the People of God.

Here is the story of how God fed the people, and how they learnt to trust in God.

Out in the hot desert there was no food to eat. Everyone began to grumble to Moses.
"What's the point of bringing us out into the desert if we are going to die of starvation?" they said.
"We were better off as slaves. At least we had food to eat in Egypt."

God listened to their complaints and said to Moses, "I will let bread rain down from heaven. Then everyone can get what they need each day."

Moses told the people what God had said.

When everyone woke in the morning, the ground was covered with something white, like frost.

"Manhu?" they all said. ("What's this?")

"This is the bread which God is giving you to eat," said Moses.

"Just collect as much as you need for today. There will be more tomorrow."

The next day there was more. It was white and sweet, like flour and honey. The people called it Manna. They were able to collect as much as they needed every day. The people lived on the Manna for the forty years they were in the desert.

New Testament

Moses was a saviour of his people, but Jesus is much greater than Moses.

Jesus is the SAVIOUR OF THE WORLD.

People loved to hear Jesus talk about God, and often they followed him out into the desert to listen to him.

Jesus was able to feed the people when they were hungry, just as Moses did.

Here is the story of the Feeding of the Five Thousand.

Great crowds used to follow Jesus because of all the people he cured. One day Jesus took a boat to a desert place, because he wanted to be alone for a while, but the people guessed where he was going and followed him there on foot. Jesus was sorry for everyone, and spent the whole day teaching them and healing the sick.

When evening came the crowds were really hungry, but there was nowhere to buy food in the desert.

Jesus' friends said, "Send the people away, so they can get some food."

Jesus said, "There is no need to send them away. YOU feed them."

The only person with any food on him was a young boy. His mother had packed a little picnic for him.

He had five small loaves of bread and two fish. The boy offered his food to the friends of Jesus. The friends took the boy to Jesus and showed him the loaves and fishes. "Here is a boy with five loaves and two fish," they said, "but that's not enough for all this crowd."

Jesus said, "Make the people sit down in groups."

When everyone sat down there were over five thousand people. Jesus took the loaves, gave thanks, and gave them out to the people. He did the same with the fish.

Everyone had as much as they wanted. When the scraps were gathered up, there were twelve baskets of food left over.

(Adapted from John 6:1-13)

Colour this picture of the boy offering his food to be shared with the crowd.

The first part of the Eucharist is called

THE LITURGY OF THE WORD.

We are going to think now about the second part of the Eucharist. This is called the

LITURGY OF THE EUCHARIST.

At the beginning of the Liturgy of the Eucharist, everything has to be prepared, just like at home everything is got ready before you eat.

(When you have received your first Holy Communion you have a chance to be an altar server. This means you can help at the Eucharist in a very special way.)

First the ALTAR is prepared.
Another word for ALTAR is
- - - - - (a b l e t)

The **PATEN** is put on the altar.
Another word for paten is
- - - - - (p a l t e)

The CHALICE is put on the altar.
Another word for chalice is
- - - (u p c)

The people bring gifts of bread and wine to be put on the altar. They also bring gifts of money earned by the work of their hands. These GIFT BEARERS stand in for everyone.
(You and your family can be gift bearers if you want to.)

The priest then says the OFFERTORY PRAYERS. These are prayers offered to God, the Lord of all Creation.

We remember that the bread and wine – and all of creation – come from God.

We also remember that people work hard in God's creation so that we have food and drink. If people didn't work together and look after the world there would be no food. We thank God for all we have. We offer our thanks and say,

BLESSED BE GOD FOR EVER

Everyday Life

Next time you have a meal, stop to think how all the food got on the table. Thank God for all you have.

Next time you go to Mass, remember to offer thanks to God for all the good things of life, and for all the people who love and care for you.

Also, remember that there are people who do not get enough to eat. What could you do for these people?

1

2

Here is a Word Search.
Find all these words.

ALTAR   CHALICE   PATEN

BREAD   WINE   OFFER

FOOD   DRINK   THANKS

```
Q A L T A R L A D O A M Y R A F
R F E H C O D T H P E F I L O R
E E F A L E C I L A H C T O X E
F W I N E V B K N T R D D L H T
F M N K R X Z W Q E T P J E G E
O T S S D R I N K N Z D A E R B
```

Remember: This is YOUR page.

Fruit of
the Vine

Everyday Life

Have you been to a party recently?
What did you have to drink there?

1. Put a tick next to the drinks you had at the party.
2. Colour in all the drinks that grown-ups might have at a party.

In most countries people like to drink on special occasions.
When they are happy they like to CELEBRATE.

Wine is often drunk at celebrations.
Wine comes from grapes. Grapes are grown in a vineyard.
Wine can make people feel very happy.
Too much wine, like too many sweets, can make you feel ill.

Children don't always like the taste of wine. It is a GROWN-UP drink.
When you were a baby, you only wanted to drink milk. As you got older
you began to eat solid food, and to have things like fizzy drinks.

Draw something you didn't drink when you were a baby, but you do
drink now.

Eventually the People of God got to the Promised Land, and settled down. Every year they had several feasts.

The most important feast was the Passover, when they remembered how God had saved them from slavery. At this feast four cups of wine were drunk.

The leader of the feast says this prayer before each cup of wine is drunk:

"Blessed are you, O Lord our God,
King of the Universe.
Creator of the fruit of the vine."

Where have you heard a prayer like this before?

Wine was such a special drink that in the Bible the People of God are called the vineyard of God. (Remember, wine comes from grapes which grow in a vineyard.)

Here is a song that Isaiah sang when the people didn't listen to the Word of God.

My friend had a
vineyard on a very rich hill.
He dug the soil and cleared it
of stones.
He planted the finest vines.
He built a tower to guard them,
dug a pit for treading the grapes.
He waited for the grapes
to ripen, but every grape
was sour.

(Isaiah 5:1-2)

Later on, Isaiah wrote this:
The Lord will say this of his
pleasant vineyard.
"I watch over it and water it all the
time. I guard it night and day so
that no one will harm it...
In days to come the people of
Israel will take root like a tree,
and they will bud. The earth will
be covered with the fruit
they produce."

(Isaiah 27:2-6)

New Testament

Jesus loved to celebrate all the Jewish feasts.

He celebrated the Sabbath every week.
He celebrated all the great yearly festivals.
He also celebrated with his friends when they got married.

Weddings were very special celebrations for the Jews. They were special for the people getting married, and they were special because the love between a man and a woman was like the love between God and the People of God.
Here is the story of the first miracle Jesus did.

One day there was a wedding in the town of Cana. Mary was invited, and so were Jesus and his friends. Everyone was having a great time, but then they ran out of wine.

Mary noticed, so she went to Jesus and said, "They have no wine left." Jesus said that it was nothing to do with him as his time hadn't come yet. Mary went to the servants and said, "Do whatever Jesus tells you to."

The Jews have lots of very strict religious rules about washing, and there were six enormous water jars standing nearby. Jesus went to the servants and said, "Fill these jars with water." The servants did what Jesus said, filled them up to the brim.

Jesus said, "Take some of the water out and give it to the head waiter to try." The servants did this, and the head waiter tasted the water. It wasn't water any more! It had all changed into wine!

The head waiter didn't realise where all the wine had come from. He went to the man getting married and said to him,

"Most people serve the best wine first, and when everyone has had plenty to drink they bring out the ordinary wine. You have kept the best wine till now."

This was the first sign that Jesus did. His friends saw how wonderful he was, and believed in him.

(Adapted from John 2:1-12)

How do you think the bride and groom felt when they ran out of wine?

What difference did Jesus make to the wedding feast?

Colour this picture of the wedding feast of Cana.

Church

When you go to the Eucharist there is so much to think about. You can think about the **PAST**. You can remember that the People of God were like a beautiful vineyard to God. We are the new People of God. We can remember how God delivers us from evil by sending us Jesus. We can be thankful for this.

Moses saved the first People of God. Jesus saves the whole world.

We can think about **NOW**. Jesus makes all the difference to our lives. Jesus makes our lives a celebration. We are the new vineyard of God. Jesus said,

"I am the vine, you are the branches."

When we are at the Eucharist we can think of everyone we know and love. We can remember that we are all joined together by love. The love of Jesus makes us all one, just as all the branches of a vine make up one plant. When we drink from the chalice at the Eucharist we can be thankful for all the good things of life, especially love and friendship.

At the Eucharist we can also think about the **FUTURE**.
Jesus often spoke about heaven as an **EVERLASTING PARTY**.
When we receive Communion we can remember that one day there will be no more sin and sorrow. We shall see God face to face, and rejoice with God and the People of God for ever and ever.

This is what that beautiful new world will be like.

Then I saw a new heaven and a new earth. I saw the Holy City, the new Jerusalem, coming down out of heaven from God, dressed like a bride ready to meet her husband. I heard a loud voice speaking from the throne: "Now God's home is with people. He will live with them, and they shall be his people. God himself will be with them, and they shall be his people. He will wipe away all tears from their eyes. There will be no more death, no more grief or crying or pain.
The old things have disappeared."

(Revelation 21:1-4)

Everyday Life

In our everyday life we often have things to celebrate. Write down three things you are thankful for.

One thing we are really thankful for is the life of Jesus. He loved us so much that he GAVE HIS LIFE for us.

When Jesus celebrated the Passover at his very **LAST SUPPER** he said the bread and wine was **HIMSELF**. The wine was his life, which he was giving for us.

Jesus called the hard times of his life a **Cup of Sorrow**.

Once he asked his friends if they could drink some of this cup with him. He said that if they could drink his cup of sorrow, they would rule with him in his kingdom. If we are strong and stand up for what is right we might find it hard at first, but in the end we will be proud of ourselves. We will see that we are bringing about God's everlasting party –

THE ETERNAL BANQUET

In the Eucharist we are united to the unselfish love of Jesus in giving up his life for his friends. "No one has greater love than to give up his life for his friends." This is exactly what Jesus did.

Here is a Word Search. Find all these words:

FEAST PARTY KINGDOM
LOVE HAPPINESS
WINE VINE BRANCHES
DRINK CUP

```
L O V E Z M H A P P I N E S S J
V C I Z Y P L K A Y T R Q W X J
K I N G D O M F R F X K N I R D
G H E M P P S W T S A E F H G D
B D F W U G H K Y L K Y T D C V
S E H C N A R B Y H J K E N I W
```

Remember: This is YOUR page. You could stick in some happy pictures of our beautiful world. You could stick in some sad pictures showing what still needs to be done to bring about the Kingdom of God.

Do this in Memory of Me

Everyday Life

We have lots of different kinds of meals.

We have [ ]
RATPIES

We have [ ]
KATE WAYAS

We have [ ]
CIPNICS

We have [ ]
CUBEBEARS

We have [ ]
MAIFLY MELAS

A really good meal is one where we enjoy the food and enjoy the company.
We are changed for the better after a really good meal.

Draw a picture of a really good meal you had. Can you remember what you ate and drank? Can you remember what you talked about?

Old Testament

We have been thinking a lot about Moses and how he led the People of God out of slavery.

At last came the great night when God finally led the people to freedom.

It was in the springtime and there was a full moon. Moses told the people to have a meal together before they went, as the journey to freedom would be long and hard.

The meal had to be eaten quickly, so there was no time to bake bread with yeast. They had to eat unleavened bread.

Each family offered a perfect young lamb to God, and ate some of it themselves.

Moses told the people they must always celebrate this PASSOVER meal. By having this meal, they would make the wonder of that night live again. It would remind them that God was their SAVIOUR, and it would make their salvation very real.

Jesus celebrated the **PASSOVER** every year. When he was a boy he asked questions about it, and learnt what it all meant.

He realised how important it was. It celebrated how the People of God were saved from sin and death. Their lives were changed from lives of slavery to lives of freedom.

Jesus spent his whole life telling people how much God loved them. It is difficult to understand that some people hated him. These people decided to kill him. Jesus knew he was going to die. The reason he had come from heaven was to give his life for us. This was how he was going to save us. By dying and rising from the dead he showed us that death and evil had no power over him, and need have no power over us. Jesus is the new

LAMB OF GOD.

Jesus didn't just give his life for us years ago when he died on Calvary. He gives us his new risen life now. He did this by changing the **Passover** feast into the **Eucharist**.

The **Eucharist** is the new **Passover** of the new People of God.

Jesus is the new Lamb of God who saves us and brings us life.

THE LAST SUPPER

The night before he died, Jesus celebrated the Passover feast with his friends. He wanted to show them how much he loved them. Judas, who was going to betray Jesus, was also there. This didn't stop Jesus from being completely full of love.

While they were at table he took bread, blessed it, broke it, and gave it to his friends. He told them to

TAKE – EAT.

THIS IS ME.

Then he took the wine. He gave thanks, and told them to share the cup. He said,

TAKE – DRINK.

THIS IS ME.

He told them to do what he had done. Whenever they did this, Jesus would be really there, as food and drink from heaven.

Colour this picture of the Last Supper.

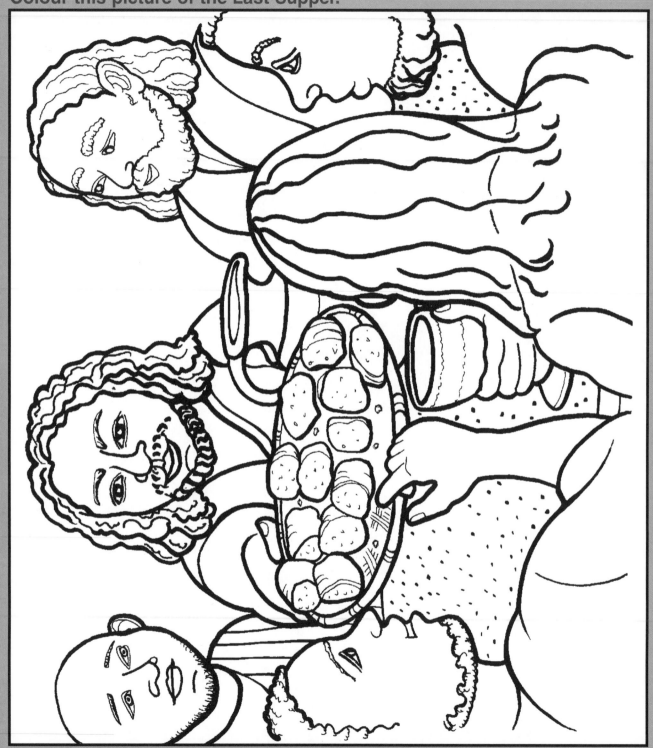

At the Eucharist the Last Supper of Jesus is taking place all over again.

The priest takes - - - - - and - - - - and says the same words that Jesus said.

TAKE AND EAT – TAKE AND DRINK. THIS IS ME.

The bread isn't ordinary bread any more. **It is Jesus – the Bread of Life.**

The wine isn't ordinary wine any more. **It is the Life of Christ.**

When we share the meal of the Eucharist we are sharing in the Life of Christ.

Jesus gives himself to us as food and drink. Why do you think he did this?

He changed bread and wine into himself because he wanted to give us his - - - - (efil)

Ordinary food and drink is very important for us because it makes us strong in our bodies.

The food and drink Jesus gives us makes us strong to

LOVE.

LOVE is the most important reason why Jesus gives us himself in the Eucharist.

• HE LOVES US.

• HE WANTS US TO LOVE HIM AND EVERYONE.

Everyday Life

If we share in the Life of Christ at the Eucharist, it means we can live like Christ every day.

You are probably trying to live loving lives already, because you are children of God.

When you receive Jesus in the Eucharist you are changed. You will have more strength for the Journey of Life, just as Moses and his people had strength for their journey to the Promised Land.

You will have more strength to love as Jesus does.

When you receive Jesus in the Eucharist you will be just as close to Jesus as his friends were at the Last Supper.

This means that no matter what problems you have to face in life, Jesus is with you. He feeds you with himself, so you have his life, his strength, his power. You have the life and love of Christ in you.

Here is a Word Search. Find all these words:

BREAD WINE TAKE
EAT PASSOVER MOSES
JESUS LAST SUPPER
CALVARY MEAL

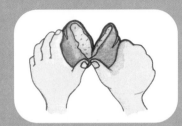

```
P L A S T S U P P E R N P S S T
V M E A L P L L R E V O S S A P
B R E A D E W G R T A K E K R K
C A L V A R Y G A G X C L A P J
B L F T U G N U D A E R E N I W
J E S U S A E A T H J S E S O M
```

REMEMBER to make this page special by adding bits of your own.

Body of
Christ

Everyday Life

Have you ever seen a tadpole turning into a frog?

First the back legs grow. Then the front legs grow.

Its long tadpole tail disappears.

Soon it can hop and live on land.

The same life is inside the little creature, but it looks completely different on the outside.

Caterpillars change as well.

At first the caterpillar is fat and crawly. It creeps along branches and twigs. Sometimes it falls to the ground.

After sleeping in a cocoon it rises to a new life as a butterfly.

Colour in this butterfly with its beautiful new wings.

You have also changed on the outside since you were born. The change in you is a gradual change. Now you are taller and stronger than when you were a baby. But you probably feel the same inside as you did a few years ago. You are the same person.

Old Testament

There are no Old Testament stories this time. Jesus came to bring about the New Testament. For Christians all the Old Testament stories are getting us ready for the New Testament. This month you are having TWO stories from the New Testament. They are both true stories about after Jesus had died and been buried. They are about

JESUS RISEN FROM THE DEAD.

New Testament

Last month we talked about the day before Jesus died. He gave himself to his friends as food and drink at his Last Supper. The next day he was put to death on the cross. This was Good Friday.

Jesus died on Good Friday. He was still dead on the Saturday. His friends were very, very sad. They thought Jesus was gone for ever. But on the third day – on the Sunday – lots of people suddenly saw him alive again. He looked so different that they did not recognise him. Here is the first story we know about Jesus appearing to someone after he had risen from the dead.

Mary and the Gardener

Mary from Magdala was very upset when Jesus died. Once she had been a very wicked woman, but she loved Jesus very much, and he had forgiven all her sins.

On the third day after Jesus had died, while it was still dark, Mary decided to go to the tomb where Jesus lay. When she got there she saw that the stone over the opening had been rolled back, and the tomb was empty. This upset her even more, because she thought the soldiers had taken away the body of Jesus.

Mary stood weeping outside the tomb. She bent down and, looking inside, saw two angels sitting there. "Why are you weeping?" they asked her. "Because they have taken Jesus away, and I don't know where he is." she sobbed.

Then she turned round, and saw someone standing there. She thought it was the gardener. The stranger asked her why she was crying. "Who are you looking for?" he said.

"Have you taken Jesus away?" she asked. The stranger looked at Mary with love. "Mary!" he said.

Straight away Mary recognised him. He wasn't a stranger. He wasn't the gardener. He was Jesus, alive with a new risen life. A better life than before.

"Master!" cried Mary, and she hugged him tightly.

She then went back to the rest of the apostles, and told them that she had seen the Lord. Jesus was alive.

(Adapted from John 20:11-18)

Mary didn't recognise Jesus because he looked very different with his new risen life.

There is another story about two friends of Jesus who didn't recognise Jesus when he rose from the dead on page 116.

Colour this picture of Jesus and Mary Magdalene.

THE TWO FRIENDS AND THE STRANGER

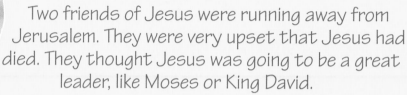

Two friends of Jesus were running away from Jerusalem. They were very upset that Jesus had died. They thought Jesus was going to be a great leader, like Moses or King David.

As they were walking along a stranger joined them, and asked what they were talking about. They told him all about Jesus dying, and how disappointed they were that Jesus had not freed the people from the Romans.

"Oh you foolish people!" said the stranger, and he began to explain the Old Testament, and how it linked up with Jesus.

The friends listened excitedly to everything the stranger said. When they got to a village they didn't want the stranger to leave them.

"Stay here with us for the night," they said. "It's getting dark." While they were at table, the stranger took bread. He blessed it and broke it and gave it to them.

All at once they recognised him. It wasn't a stranger. It was Jesus – alive with his new risen life.

As soon as they recognised him Jesus disappeared. But the friends were no longer afraid. "We should have guessed," they said. "All the time he was talking to us along the road our hearts were burning inside us. Jesus looks different on the outside with his new risen life, but inside it is the very same Jesus."

Straight away the two friends hurried back to Jerusalem, and joined the rest of the friends there. "It is true," everyone said. "Jesus has really risen from the dead."

(Adapted from Luke 24:13-35)

When we go to the Eucharist we really and truly meet Jesus, just as Mary Magdalene did, and just as the two friends did.

Jesus isn't there with a physical body, like the one he had before he died, but we really do meet him in a special way when we go to Communion.

It is the same Jesus, who died for us and rose again, but he is with us by the power of the Holy Spirit, who makes Jesus present in the bread and wine.

When the priest says the words of Consecration,

"THIS IS MY BODY"
"THIS IS THE CUP OF MY BLOOD"

the Holy Spirit enters the bread and wine with the risen life of Christ.

When we receive the bread the priest says,

"THE BODY OF CHRIST."

We say,

"AMEN."

(Yes, we believe.)

When we receive the cup the priest says,

"THE BLOOD OF CHRIST."

We say,

"AMEN."

(Yes, we believe.)

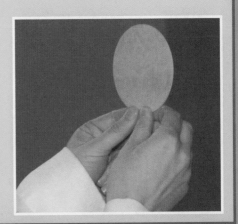

Everyday Life

When we receive Jesus in Holy Communion we are united with him in a very special way.

We are all so close to him that we become the Body of Christ. This means that although on the outside we may look just the same as before, by receiving Holy Communion we are changed. We have the risen life of Christ in us.

WE ARE THE BODY OF CHRIST.

Jesus still had the marks of his wounds when he rose from the dead. After receiving the Eucharist we may feel wonderful, we may feel ordinary or we may feel we are weak and wounded. Just because we are the new Body of Christ doesn't make us perfect.

But no matter how you feel when you receive Jesus in the Eucharist, you know that he is deep inside your being. He loves you even more than you can possibly realise.

After receiving Jesus, try to keep still and quiet. You can talk to him in your own words, or just enjoy recognising he is with you.

Finish this prayer.

Dear Jesus,
thank you for coming to me in the
Eucharist...

Next time we meet, we will be thinking about all we can do to carry on the Good News that Jesus gives us.

For now, here is a Word Search. Find all these words.

CHANGE RECOGNISE BELIEVE

RISEN LIFE FAITH

SPIRIT AMEN CHRIST

E V E I L E B Q W C H R I S T R
H Y G T I R I P S G H J K L P P
Q W N Z X I W N B X S S E D H J
F K A B V S Z M B H T I A F T R
H J H M N E X L K X C Z W Q I W
R E C O G N I S E G J N E M A L

Make this page special by adding bits of your own.

To Love and to Serve

Everyday Life

Every day you are lucky enough to have something to eat.
Draw your favourite food and drink.

If you don't eat you feel - - - - (weka)

You might even - - - - - (fanit)

Draw you feeling weak before a meal and full of energy after a meal.

Me feeling weak before a meal.   Me full of energy after a meal.

We have spent a long time thinking about how Moses helped the People of God escape from slavery. In the desert the people were fed by God to give them strength for the journey.

At last they reached the Promised Land. Joshua was the leader by then, so Joshua led the people to freedom. Joshua is the same name as Jesus. The name means

SAVIOUR

The People of God settled in the Promised Land. It was so wonderful after the desert that they said it was a land flowing with milk and honey. There was plenty to eat and drink for everyone. The People of God always tried to be kind to poor people and to strangers. They remembered that once they had been poor travellers, with nowhere to live. When they forgot to think of others, the prophets reminded them.

Jesus is a prophet, but he is much more than a prophet.

Jesus is the

SON OF GOD

New Testament

Jesus, the Son of God, spent his life on earth showing us how to live as children of God. Jesus was always kind to the poor people. He healed the sick, fed the hungry, he told everyone how much God loved them.

After he rose from the dead he carried on loving everyone. Here is a story of how he fed his friends when they were tired and hungry.

One evening Peter was bored. He said to his friends, "I'm going fishing." His friends said, "We'll come with you." They got their old boat out, and dragged it into the lake. They fished all night, but they couldn't catch anything. Not even an old sandal!

When the sunrise came they were cold and hungry. They decided to go home. They were very disappointed. Now they would have to buy some food for their breakfast. They could see a stranger on the shore. The stranger called out to them, "Have you caught anything?" "No," they called back to the stranger. "Cast your net on the other side of the boat," shouted the stranger. "Then you will find some fish."

They cast their net, and to their surprise, they caught so many fish that they could not pull the net on board. "It's the Lord!" shouted John. When Peter heard this, he jumped overboard to get to Jesus. When everyone else had landed, they noticed that Jesus had a fire already lit, and he was cooking a lovely breakfast for them on the beach.

Jesus took the bread and gave it to them. He gave them some fish. They knew it was Jesus feeding them. Then Jesus asked Peter three times if he loved him. Peter said yes, and Jesus told him to feed his lambs and sheep.

(Adapted from John 21:1-17)

The lambs and sheep of Jesus are all the poor, weak people of the world. Jesus asks his friends to look after them all.

Colour this picture of Jesus with food for his friends at the seaside.

At the end of the Eucharist, the minister says,

"Go in peace to love and serve the Lord."
Go out to love and serve the Lord. We have been fed by our Good Shepherd.
Now we have a chance to show how much we love him. We have a chance to
copy him, by loving and serving everyone we meet.

"Here are some ways you can love and serve
the Lord during the week:"

help someone older than you

do the gardening

look after baby

visit someone sick

Write a letter to your Prayer Sponsor saying thank you for praying for you.
Here is some help with ideas and spelling.

Dear ....

Thank you very much for praying for me.

enjoyed First Holy Communion lovely weather excited
nervous very happy family relations presents tired

I hope you are keeping well

Love

Here is your last Word Search. Have fun doing it, and enjoy belonging to the New People of God for the rest of your life. The words you are looking for are

HAPPINESS CHRIST CONTENTMENT STRENGTH

LORD LIFE LOVE

```
H A P P I N E S S C H R I S T L
H Y G T L R I P E G H J K L O O
S W N H T G N E R T S S E V H R
S K R B V S Z M V H T I E F T D
P D H M N E X L E X C Z W Q I W
M E T N E M T N E T N O C M A L
```

THANKS BE TO GOD

Make this page special by adding bits of your own. You could add pages and pages of things if you wanted to. It could be a place where you collect prayers and ideas about God and people and everything God has made.

My Prayers

Sign of the Cross
In the name of the Father,
and of the Son,
and of the Holy Spirit.
Amen.

The Lord's Prayer
Our Father, who art in heaven,
hallowed be thy name;
thy kingdom come;
thy will be done on earth as it is in
heaven.
Give us this day our daily bread;
and forgive us our trespasses
as we forgive those
who trespass against us;
and lead us not into temptation,
but deliver us from evil.
Amen.

Hail Mary

Hail, Mary, full of grace,
the Lord is with you.
Blessed are you among women,
and blessed is the fruit
of your womb, Jesus.
Holy Mary, Mother of God,
pray for us sinners,
now and at the hour of our death.
Amen.

Glory be to the Father

Glory be to the Father and to the Son and to the Holy Spirit,
as it was in the beginning, is now, and ever shall be,
world without end.
Amen.

Grace before Meals

Thank you, Lord, for this food
and for the work of those who prepared it.
Bless us as we share your gifts.
Amen.

Prayer of Thanksgiving

Thank you, Lord, for all your gifts to me.
Help me to use them in your service.
Amen.

The Apostles' Creed
I believe in God, the Father almighty,
creator of heaven and earth.
I believe in Jesus Christ, his only Son, our Lord,
who was conceived by the Holy Spirit,
born of the Virgin Mary,
suffered under Pontius Pilate,
was crucified, died, and was buried;
he descended to the dead.
On the third day he rose again;
he ascended into heaven,
is seated at the right hand of the Father,
and will come again to judge the living and the dead.
I believe in the Holy Spirit,
the holy catholic Church,
the communion of saints,
the forgiveness of sins,
the resurrection of the body,
and life everlasting.
Amen.

Eucharistic Responses

Penitential Rite

Priest: …Lord, have mercy.
People: Lord, have mercy.
Priest: …Christ, have mercy.
People: Christ, have mercy.
Priest: …Lord, have mercy.
People: Lord, have mercy.

Liturgy of the Word

After the first reading:
Priest: This is the Word of the Lord.
People: Thanks be to God.
Before the gospel:
Priest: The Lord be with you.
People: And also with you.
Priest: A reading from the holy gospel according to…
People: Glory to you, Lord.
After the reading of the gospel:
Priest: This is the gospel of the Lord.
People: Praise to you, Lord Jesus Christ.

The Sign of Peace

Priest: The peace of the Lord be with you always.
People: And also with you.
The priest invites the people to give the sign of peace.
Priest: Let us offer each other the sign of peace.
At Mass we exchange a sign of peace by shaking hands with those around us and by saying: Peace be with you.

Eucharistic Acclamation

Priest: ...Let us proclaim the mystery of faith:

People: Christ has died,
Christ is risen,
Christ will come again.

or

People: Dying you destroyed our death,
rising you restored our life,
Lord Jesus, come in glory.

or

People: When we eat this bread
and drink this cup,
we proclaim your death, Lord Jesus,
until you come in glory.

or

People: Lord, by your cross and resurrection
you have set us free.
You are the Saviour of the world.

Rite of Communion

People: Lord, I am not worthy to receive
you, but only say the word and I
shall be healed.

Dismissal

Priest: Go in peace to love and serve the Lord.

People: Thanks be to God.

Special Words

Baptism ~ At my baptism I became a member of God's Christian family, the Church.

Body of Christ ~ A name for Holy Communion and also a name for the family of the Church.

Bread of Life ~ A name for the sacrament of Jesus in Holy Communion.

Eucharist ~ means thanksgiving.

*At the Last Supper Jesus asked us to **"Do this in memory of me"**.*

Jesus took bread and wine, he blessed it, he broke the bread and gave the bread and wine to his disciples to eat and drink.

When we gather together to celebrate the Eucharist we do what Jesus asked us to do: we take the gifts of bread and wine, we bless them, the priest breaks the bread, and at Communion he gives us Jesus under the appearance of bread and wine.

Eucharistic Prayer ~ The prayer which is at the heart of the Mass when our gifts of bread and wine are blessed and we are reminded that Jesus lived, died, and rose from the dead so that we can share his life for ever.

Gospel ~ The Good News of Jesus Christ.

Holy Communion ~ This is the moment when we receive Jesus under the appearance of bread and wine.

Host ~ The wafer of bread which is consecrated by the priest in the Eucharistic Prayer.

Lamb of God ~ A name Christians give to Jesus.

Last Supper ~ The special meal which Jesus shared with his friends the night before he died.

Liturgy of the Word ~ The part of the Mass when we listen to readings from the Bible.

Preparation of Gifts ~ The time during the Eucharist when we prepare and bring gifts of bread and wine forward in procession to offer as signs of our world which are to be changed into the sacrament of Jesus present in a special way amongst us.

Sign of Peace ~ A sign of love and friendship, usually a handshake, by which we wish one another the peace of Christ.

MEMO

These people were present to celebrate my First Communion Day with me

I received Holy Communion for the first time on

_____

at

_____

Celebrant

_____

My catechist

_____

My parent/s

_____

I Belong
First Holy Communion Programme

Published by Redemptorist Publications

Text: Aileen Urquhart
Additional text: Jill Talbot-Ponsonby

Illustration and Design: Lis Davis

Copyright © Redemptorist Publications
Published by Redemptorist Publications, a Registered Charity Limited by guarantee.
Registered in England 3261721

First published March 1998
Revised edition August 2002
Reprinted April 2006

ISBN 0 85231 171 0

Printed and bound in China through Colorcraft Ltd., Hong Kong.

Redemptorist
PUBLICATIONS

Alphonsus House, Chawton, Hampshire GU34 3HQ
Telephone 01420 88222   Fax 01420 88805
rp@rpbooks.co.uk   www.rpbooks.co.uk